HOMES

by Robin Nelson

first step nonfiction

Lerner Publications Company · Minneapolis

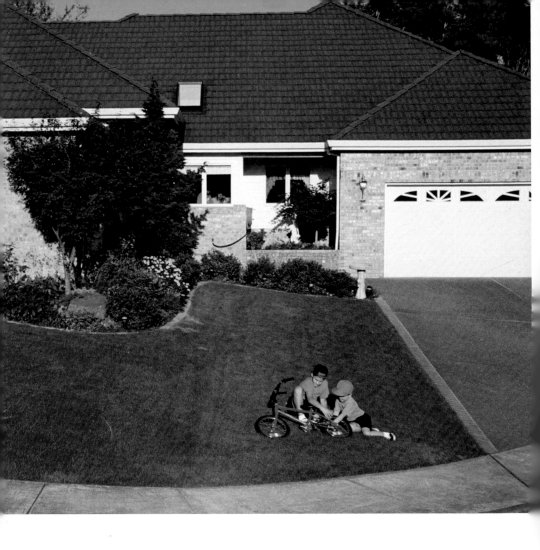

Everyone needs a home.

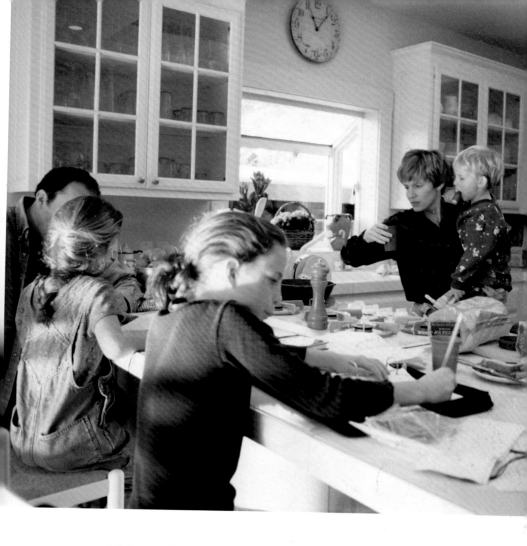

We live in our home.

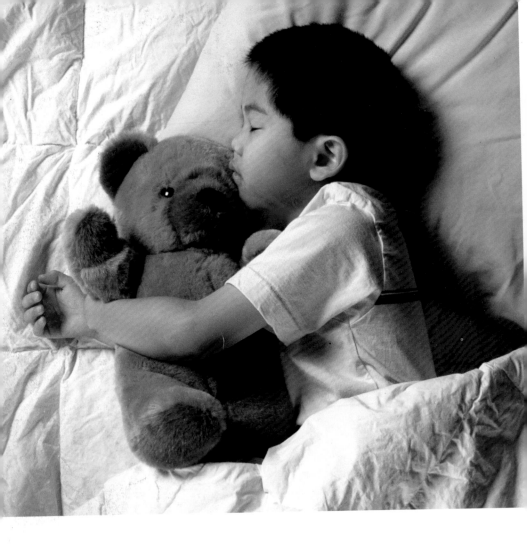

We sleep in our home.

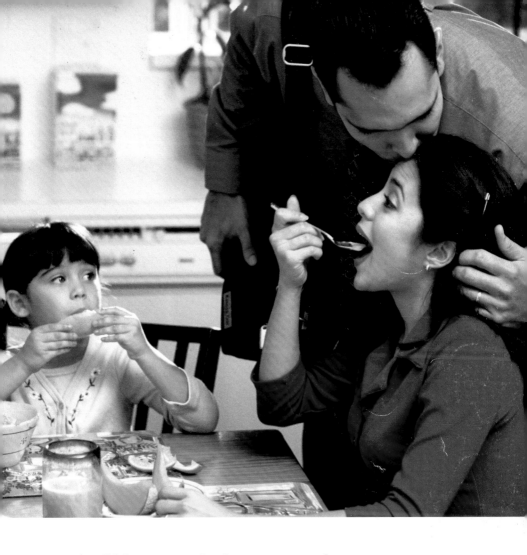

We eat in our home.

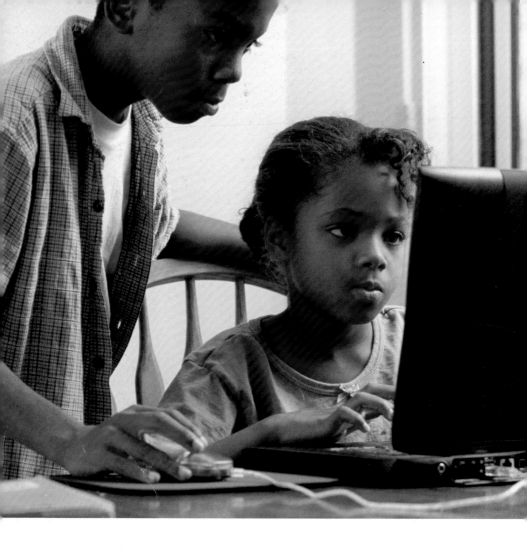

We work in our home.

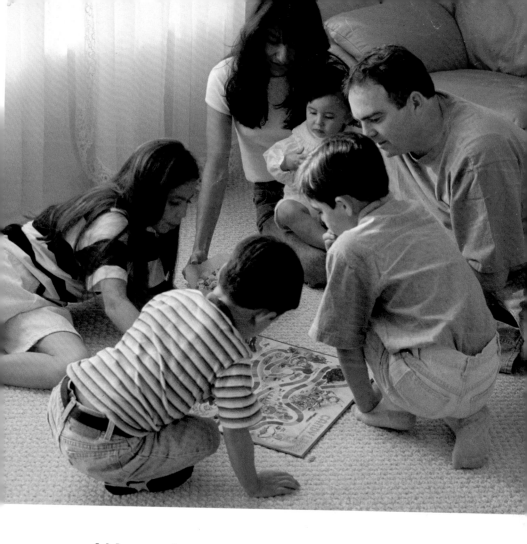

We play in our home.

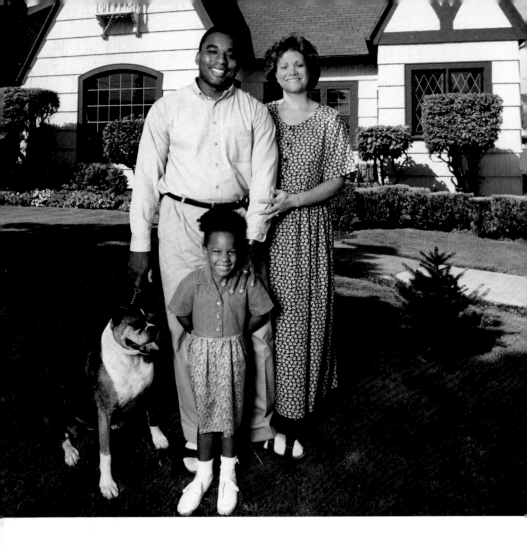

We all need a home.